THE MYSTICAL KNOWLEDGE OF GOD

AN ESSAY IN THE ART OF KNOWING AND LOVING THE DIVINE MAJESTY BY DOM SAVINIEN LOUISMET O.S.B.

TO MARY IMMACULATE
MOTHER OF BEAUTIFUL
LOVE THIS LITTLE
TREATISE IS HUMBLY
& LOVINGLY DEDICATED

PREFACE

THE present work is a treatise on the experimental knowledge o God, such as it is possible for every Christian to acquire, if he will but do what is needful thereto. The reader must not expect to find in these few pages the whole doctrine of the mystic life, nor even of mental prayer, as such; still less must he look for an exposition of the extraordinary and miraculous dealings of God with a few favoured souls. I may attempt these higher themes later on, God willing; but in the present work my aim is purely and simply to show that every Christian can obtain a most beautiful kind of knowledge of God, and enlarge it, by the practice of love. It is the substance of a series of sermons, preached by me from time to time at Buckfast, reduced to a body of doctrine for the more convenient use of myself, and those under my spiritual guidance. I have been persuaded to give it to the public at large, in the hope that it may do good.

In the pulpit it was natural to speak "tanquam potestatem habens," as one having a divine mandate to fulfil. In these pages I have not much departed from the same homiletic or hortatory style, judging it to suit the purpose of the work. We cannot improve upon the Fathers of the Church, from, let us say, Dyonisius the Areopagite, down to St. Francis of Sales: in my opinion a grievous mistake has been made in giving to works of piety too didactic a form.

No one need be frightened by the bulk of this treatise; eight short chapters conclude it all. It could be read at one sitting, though in order to benefit from it, it would be more profitable to have it, and read it again and again. Its very conciseness will make this a light task.

In Part 1. I endeavour to set before

the reader the reality and the true nature of the mystical knowledge of God. In Part II. I treat of the enlargement of the same. Even this second part, if attentively considered, will be seen to be nothing more than a further illustration, and a deeper one, of what is meant by this precious, experimental knowledge of God.

The substance of this work appeared first in the "Catholic Review of July and October, 1915.

THE TABLE OF CONTENTS

PREFACE

EPILOGUE

PART I. OF THE NATURE OF MYSTICAL KNOWLEDGE

"Our good Lord showed me that it is full great pleasure to Him, that a silly soul come to Him naked, plainly and homely."
Juliana of Norwich.

CHAPTER I

ON THE KNOWLEDGE OF GOD IN GENERAL

KNOWLEDGE, a rational, intelligent knowledge of things, is a mark of man's nobility. Beasts have some kind of knowledge, imperfect and limited, unreasoning, and purely material. Man knows himself by his intellect, as also his fellow-men, the world around him, the sciences, the arts, history ; he may even know the "invisible," that which is not apprehended by the senses ; and he may know God Himself, and this last knowledge is the greatest, the most useful, the most necessary of all. It is, in fact, of such fundamental importance that Holy Writ tells us *they are vain in whom there is not the knowledge of God* (Wisdom xiii. 1). They are vain—i.e., useless, unprofitable alike to themselves and the world; they are good for nothing, when not positively harmful.

In Heaven we shall know God perfectly. We shall see Him even as He is and face to face, He himself being the Light that will enlighten us; we shall know even as we are known. It is not so now; we see Him but imperfectly and dimly as through a veil, yet, from the very nature of its object, even this imperfect knowledge of God is the most excellent and the most necessary of all. Alas! it is a knowledge which is rare—few there are that seek it, few desire or realize its inestimable worth. Men make great efforts to learn of things new and strange and curious, but for the things of God they seem to have no care. It is as though men thought God was of no interest, nor the knowledge of Him worth troubling about. How blind, how foolish, are they, for is it not self-evident, on the contrary, that God is the most interesting object of knowledge of all —the most enthralling, the most absorbing?

There are three ways of gaining a certain knowledge of God whilst we are yet on earth: the first is by natural reason; the second, by faith; the third, by love.

The first kind of knowledge of God is called philosophical.

From the consideration of himself and of the universe it is possible for a man, even without the help of supernatural grace, to arrive at the certainty of the existence of God and at the unity and infinite perfection of God—i.e., man is able, by the light of reason, alone and unaided, to assure himself that there is a Supreme Being, that there is but One, that He is full of the most magnificent perfections, a pure Spirit, supremely good, and wise, and happy ; free, intelligent, and personal, distinct from and independent of the universe, first cause of all things, holding absolute dominion over all ; and that we men, as free agents and His creatures, are responsible to Him for all we do.

Let us suppose, for instance, that a man had never heard of God—a man of clear intellect, and one blinded by no passions. By applying his mind to the consideration of himself and the world around him, such a man could arrive at this knowledge of God.

The pagan philosophers of old had this speculative rational knowledge of God, and if they had followed it up they would have attained His sacred Love, for it is of faith that God never denies His grace to those who seek Him.

Those pagans, therefore, as St. Paul (Rom. i., 20) says, are inexcusable, who, leading evil lives, lost their souls, for they knew God, but, failing to give Him due honour, they were debarred from His grace.

Yet more inexcusable are those men of our own time who refuse to acknowledge the very existence of God. What the pagans could find without the light of Christianity, they surely can find now, if they are willing to seek it.

Likewise inexcusable are those who acknowledge the existence of God, and yet refuse to give Him the homage they know to be His due.

The second kind of knowledge of God is by way of faith. It is ministered to us by divine revelation contained in Holy Scripture, and in the divine Tradition of the Catholic Church. These are summarised for us in the Creed and in the Catechism, and are propounded at greater length in the works of the Fathers and orthodox theologians.

Take, for example, a child who has never seen his father because his father has gone to a distant country. The father writes to his dear son letters full of tender and delicate affection, and little by little informs the son of many things about himself that will interest him. The child in this way, though he has never seen the father, becomes possessed of much knowledge concerning him. In what way? By faith: by believing what his father writes to him. Now, God has done as much for us. Separated in a way from us by the conditions of our present life, God is living in a far-away country we call Heaven, and He has written letters to us, and sent us messengers and messages.

The prophets of old were the messengers of God to mankind. Occasionally He sent His very Angels, and in the fullness of time He sent His own Son, clothed in our humanity. The burden of the message, of which all these were the bearers, has been consigned to Holy Writ, or handed down by divine tradition. Thus the one and the other are nothing else than letters from God to man, teaching him of things which he could not have found out by the natural powers of unassisted reason.

We learn about God Himself, first of all, that, though He is One in Essence, He is a Trinity of Persons — Father, Son, and Holy Ghost. We shall see, later on, that this knowledge gives us an insight into the very life of God.

Then we are made to know explicitly His great works *ad extra*, viz., that He created the visible and invisible world out of nothing. That He made all things for His own glory, and rules them infallibly to this end by His Providence. That He made the Angels and then man to His own image and likeness. That He tried the Angels, of whom one-third were found wanting—and became devils. That He tried man, and that in this trial the whole race fell in Adam (Mary alone being preserved), whence it follows that every man that enters into the world does so with the stain of sin and all the consequences of sin upon his soul.

We are taught that, nevertheless, God so loved mankind as to give His only Son for its ransom; and how the wonderful love of the Son was manifested in the Incarnation. That fallen man was redeemed by the Cross. That men of goodwill

8

are sanctified by the Sacraments of the Church. And, finally, that the elect will be glorified in Heaven by the beatific vision, and the reprobate will be damned to the fire of hell, separated from God for all eternity.

Now, all these things could not have come to our knowledge by the light of natural reason alone. It was necessary that they should be revealed to us—they have been so revealed, and it is by faith in this revelation that we come to a higher and a greater knowledge of God. How magnificent, how fatherly, how very near to us does God appear in the light of revelation! Let us be thankful for the knowledge it has given us, let us try to appreciate it to the full!

But this is not the end—there is yet a higher knowledge within our grasp. This is the mystical knowledge of God, the peculiar knowledge we gain by love—by active, conscious and constant love of Him. This is a personal, experimental knowledge of God, which every Christian can obtain by the help of grace, and God does not deny His grace to those that seek it. He desires to impart the grace of this knowledge to each one of us if we will but let Him.

CHAPTER II
ON THE MYSTICAL KNOW-LEDGE OF GOD BY LOVE

WE have seen that there are three ways of gaining a certain knowledge of God while we are yet on earth. The first is by natural reason, the second by faith, the third by love ; and we have seen what is meant by the first two kinds of knowledge of God. Many go no further than this. Through their own negligence and carelessness they never come to the third kind of knowledge of God, by the way of fervent love. This is a thousand pities, for they deprive themselves of a great good, and at the same time refuse to God a satisfaction He has every right to expect. It is this third kind of knowledge of God I will now proceed to describe, so that those who have it not may be awakened to the necessity and desirability of acquiring it.

The first and most important thing about the way of the knowledge of God by love is that it is experimental. Experimental knowledge is that attained by seeing, hearing, touching, or in any way soever coming into contact with, or being united to, the object of which we seek to learn, whereby we make certain proof of this object and of its attributes. If a person had never tasted honey, but had been told that it was sweet, and had read a great deal upon the subject of honey, he would have a certain knowledge of it, but not an experimental one. But let him taste the honey, actually put it in his mouth, and let it melt there, and feel the sensation of delight it gives him, then only will he know how sweet it was; he will have proved its sweetness and acquired an experimental knowledge of it.

Knowledge of God by the way of love is of the same order. *Taste and see that the Lord is sweet* (Ps. xxxiii., 9).

Let us take another example of experimental knowledge to illustrate our point — that of the poor Samaritan woman we read about in the Gospel of St. John, with whom Our Lord engaged in conversation at the well of Jacob. She was so struck by what He told her that she ran into the city, as one beside herself, crying out : " Come and see a man who has told me all I have done. Come and see if He is not the Messiah." No doubt the good people marvelled at first at the woman's description of Our Lord. How gentle He was and how saintly He appeared ; how His words had pierced her heart and strangely moved her. . . . Then they came to Our Lord and saw Him, and spoke to

Him and heard Him. They begged Him to come down to their city, and He did so, showing Himself to them all, the great Teacher, the great Healer, the great Consoler. He stayed with them two days, and many believed in Him because of His Word, and they said to the woman: " We now believe, not for thy saying, for we ourselves have heard Him, and know that this is indeed the Saviour of the world." Note these words: " We ourselves have heard Him." Here we have experimental knowledge. Such is the knowledge of God by love.

Yet another illustration of experimental knowledge. A little child is at his mother's breast, in her arms. Does he know his own mother? Assuredly he knows her. How does he know her? Experimentally. His knowledge is not a rational knowledge, he has not the use of reason; neither is it knowledge by faith or hearsay. If one were to tell the child this was his mother he would not understand, but he finds himself in her arms, pressed fondly to her bosom, and he knows. He feels himself loved, and instinctively, in his feeble way, he returns love for love and caress for caress. If he is taken away from her he cries and holds out tiny hands, for he has no peace until he finds himself once more in the arms of her who is all the world to him. Who will say the child knows not his mother? He could not speak learnedly about her, nor describe her, but he knows that she is sweet; he has proved it for himself, and he would not change her for the whole world. Now, this again is experimental knowledge—the sort of knowledge of God which the fervent soul gains by the way of love.

The loving soul finds herself in the arms and on the warm breast, if I may so speak, of this more than mother, the good God, and she loves to be there. She takes her sole delight in God, and the more she does so the more God presses her to His heart, and secretly manifests Himself to her, letting her taste and see how sweet He is. That soul may be very illiterate, may not be able to discourse very learnedly about God, may be very deficient in philosophical and theological acumen ; but who can say that she does not know God ? She has the very best knowledge of Him, the knowledge He Himself gives her personally and immediately. She has been able to make proof of God, and she has found Him very sweet indeed.

Yes, to the soul of good will, who allows God to have His own way,

God gives Himself to be known thus by experimental knowledge. He communicates immediately to such a soul the sense of His own sweetness. He is in her mouth as a lump of honey, slowly dissolving into unutterable sweetness. He is in the midst of that soul, even as He was in the Samaritan village all affability, and kindness, and consolation, allowing Himself to be approached and touched & familiarly spoken to. He takes the soul, even as the mother takes her child, lovingly into the arms of His affection and feeds her at the breasts of His infinite tenderness.

Now that we know that the knowledge of God by the way of love is experimental, it is easy for us to tell whether we possess it or not. Do you experience at times in the secret of your heart the delightful sweetness of spiritual consolation ? Then have no sort of doubt, it is God making Himself known to you. Do you at times feel Him very near indeed, His presence in the midst of your soul, and at such times is ·He not like a loving friend come unto his own, one in whose presence you are very much at ease? And does He not then bring with Him a joy that is not of this world? Then have no sort of doubt, it is God giving you to taste and see how sweet He is. Do you experience from time to time the feeling of perfect peace and security, even in the midst of dryness and internal trials, as of one leaning on the very breast of God? And do you, in this reliance on God, find joy even in the midst of tribulations? Then you have indeed that experimental knowledge of God which comes only by love.

If, on the contrary, we know for certain that God exists, because everybody says so, and our reason tells us it must be so, and if by the same process and the teaching of Holy Writ and the Church we come by the knowledge of His goodness, but without any personal inward experience of it, then our knowledge is only by way of reason or faith, but not by the way of love. It is not yet all that God would have it to be. God has not yet been able to make Himself known to us, for we are not such as He would have us be, He cannot yet let us taste and see how sweet He is.

But the fault is our own; we have not loved. Let us begin to love God as He would be loved. Let us now love Him with our whole heart and soul and above all things; not the world or some idol or ourselves instead of Him, but only God Himself. Then he will come to us and manifest Himself and let us taste and see how sweet He is.

19

CHAPTER III

THE TESTIMONY OF GOD CONCERNING THIS KNOWLEDGE

FROM what has been said it may be inferred that knowledge of God by reason or by faith is an indirect knowledge, from a distance and from without, whilst knowledge of God by love is knowledge at once close, immediate, and from within. It is an infusion of divine light and sweetness and strength, direct from God into the soul, without passing through the channel of outward sight or symbol, such as the Sacred Scriptures, or the Sacraments, or the ministrations of men. Knowledge by reason and faith is good, but the mystical knowledge of God is better, giving more honour to God and bringing more profit to the soul.

The question may be raised: Is such a knowledge of God really given to men on earth? Does God really give Himself to be known by an intimate secret contact with the loving soul? Or is it all imagination on the part of the mystic, or, as scientists have it, auto-suggestion? Is there no illusion in it?

The answer is easy. We have, on the one hand, the testimony of God in Holy Scripture, repeated, emphatic, and explicit; and, on the other, that of all true lovers of God, the canonized Saints, the Doctors of the Church, and the mystics. They one and all affirm that such knowledge is attainable and obtainable by men on earth, even by every man, as we shall see later.

What is the testimony of God concerning it? Apart from the many beautiful passages of the Old Testament, the Moral Books, the Prophets, and the Canticle of Canticles, let us confine ourselves to what Our Lord says. He is God Himself, the Master of the Mystical Life. He tells us that He does impart such knowledge, and also the conditions necessary for its reception.

Our Lord says (Matt. v. 8) : *Blessed are the pure in heart, for they shall see God.* All the commentators are agreed that the meaning of this passage is not only that the pure in heart may count upon the vision of God in the future life in Heaven, but that they shall, in a manner, see God, even during their pilgrimage upon earth. In what way? Thus: they shall have a perception of God, personal, experimental, of a kind that is denied those that are not pure. And to him who does not understand this mystical higher knowledge of God, and who is inclined to be sceptical, I would say, " Friend, is your heart pure ? Are you clean in thought and speech, and deed and affection ? If not, there is the difficulty. You cannot hope to understand until you are pure in heart." *Animalis homo non percipit ea quae Spiritus Dei sunt* (Cor. ii. 14), the poor sinner, the slave of lusts, cannot have any perception of these things. Therefore, let those who desire not only to understand, but to taste and see how sweet the Lord is, become pure in heart. They will then begin to attain to this higher or mystical knowledge of God.

Our Lord says again (Jn. xiv. 21) : *If a man loveth Me, I will manifest Myself to him.* Here it is evident that He speaks of that special manifestation of Himself that comes to a man not by reasoning but by love. It is here no longer question of that official revelation which he has made to all men through the Church, but of a personal favour done to the soul, of that near and immediate contact by which He gives His faithful servant to taste of His sweetness. The words bear no other interpretation: "I will manifest Myself to him"—i.e., I will show Myself to him in a direct and intimate manner, and this cannot but be very sweet. It is obvious that God should reserve for those who love Him a knowledge of Himself more intimate and precious and delightful than that which is vouchsafed to the sinner. Even the most perverse sinner may have a purely speculative knowledge of God, such as is supplied by study of philosophy and theology.

In another place (Luke x. 21), Our Lord says: *I give Thee thanks, O Father, Lord of heaven and earth, because Thou hast hidden these things from the wise and prudent and hast revealed them to little ones.* Here He informs us that there are things which God is pleased to reveal to little ones— i.e., to all those who by humility become little in their own estimation, whilst He keeps that very particular knowledge back from those who are proud of their learning or natural powers. Now, what are the things thus revealed ? What is that knowledge of God which is denied to the philosopher and even to the learned theologian, if he be not a little child in humility ? It cannot be any other than the higher knowledge, the immediate, personal, experimental knowledge of God, God giving Himself to be tasted by the loving, humble, child-like soul.

Many more quotations from the Gospel and the Apocalypse could be cited, all as forceful and explicit as those we have used, to show that the experimental knowledge of God is no pious fiction, no invention of over-zealous, illusioned devotees.

Amen, I say to you, whosoever shall not receive the Kingdom of God as a little child shall not enter therein (Mark x. 15). How does the little child receive the Gospel from the lips of its mother, or the good Sisters or the Priest? With the utmost simplicity and the greatest confidence. He does not reason about it, or find fault with it, or take this and reject that. No. If we were to go to our children's class at Catechism, we should see how the child receives the truths told to him. There would be no modernism there. Is this folly on the part of the child? Far from it. With the grace of his baptism still fresh upon him, and his natural innocence helping, he will give a rational, earnest and honest assent to all that is told him. The child draws his conclusions strictly. He would be astonished if he were told not to love God, or only to love Him a little. A child is uncompromising in his reception of the Kingdom of God. There was a time when we were such ourselves, but, alas ! many years ago. We were once little children, and received the Kingdom of God in simplicity, and we desired to love our Master with our whole heart. We have grown indeed, but in worldly wisdom, and the unquestioning and undivided love we vowed to God when we were little has been scattered to the winds. We found it would cost us a great effort, and a lifelong one, to love God as we should, to keep on loving Him as children do, so we compromised the matter. We no longer receive and retain the Kingdom of God, the Gospel teach-

27

ing, "as a little child," and so we cannot penetrate therein. This Kingdom of God on earth, which is the mystical life, the knowledge of God by love, the enjoyment of Him and the marvellous sanctification of the soul consequent thereto, are denied us, because the conditions necessary to their acquirement are lacking in us. *Amen, I say to you, whosoever shall not receive the Kingdom of God as a little child shall not enter therein.*

The First Commandment is, *Thou shalt love the Lord thy God.* Jesus did not say, " Thou shalt understand the Lord thy God, or thou shalt be learned about Him," only, " Thou shalt love." And He tells us how to do this. *With thy whole heart, with thy whole soul, with thy whole mind, with thy whole strength.* Thus only may we hope to gain the mystical knowledge of God, to taste and see how sweet the Lord is. The invitation, or rather command, is not to a few, not to a select class or to His Apostles only, but to all men. All are invited, but how few, how very few, come to the feast!

We have seen that this special experimental knowledge of God, with its wonderful sweetness, is given to souls of good will. We know also the conditions necessary for attaining it. They are purity of heart, humility, and holy simplicity, virtues attendant on the true love of God.

Beyond this there is no greater or higher knowledge, excepting that vouchsafed the blessed in heaven, in the beatific vision.

CHAPTER IV

NO POSSIBILITY OF DELUSION IN THE MYSTICAL KNOWLEDGE OF GOD BY LOVE

WHEN we say that God makes Himself known in a special manner to the loving soul, that He manifests Himself to the mystic, people are apt to imagine this to mean that God shows Himself to the mystic in visions and revelations. Or, again, they confuse this inward secret manifestation which God makes to the soul with the well-known phenomenon of sensible or sentimental devotion. Now we must well understand that the experimental knowledge of God by love is neither a kind of miraculous apparition nor the suspicious sweetness of sensible devotion, and it is subject to no possible delusion.

Sensible fervour may come almost to anyone, saint or sinner, and from a variety of causes—even such as have hardly anything to do with the love of God. It may come occasionally to a tepid or negligent Christian upon witnessing some unusual display of religious pomp and ceremony, or on hearing a fine voice, or music beautifully rendered. This is but a shallow, passing impression on the surface of the soul, or, rather, in the region of the senses and imagination. Nevertheless, it is a grace of God in its way, and the Christian will do well to heed it, and make it the starting point of a more fervent life. If he fail to do so, there is a danger that this brief period of sensible fervour be followed by a depressing sense of loneliness and desolation, and a temptation to abandon the whole enterprise of the spiritual life. From this it is plain that a fit of sensible fervour is not a manifestation of God Himself, made by Him directly into the soul. Therefore this must not be taken for the mystical knowledge of God, which, as we have said, is just such a manifestation of God, by God, directly into the soul. Nor does it consist in visions, revelations, and ecstasies such as certain saints have been favoured with; nor, again, some miraculous and definite setting before the eyes of the mystic of some form or image of the Divine essence.

In this matter of visions and revelations, delusions are easy. Visions may come from God or they may not. We read in Holy Scripture that the devil has power to change himself, seemingly, into an angel of light, and to work upon the senses and imagination and thus deceive even the saints. Saint Simeon Stylites, after he had

been many years on his column, was
visited by a cherub driving a fiery
chariot, who told him that God had
need of him in paradise. Simeon was
about to mount the fiery chariot, but
before doing so he was inspired to
make the sign of the Cross. Upon
this the whole thing fell to earth with
a crash. It had been nothing but a
snare of the evil spirit.

Hundreds of examples might be
cited to show that visions and revelations, seemingly the most trustworthy,
may be nothing but the work of the
spirit of darkness and most dangerous
delusions. This is why all spiritual
writers warn us that visions, ecstasies,
and revelations may never be desired
or prayed for, and that when they
come unbidden they must be received
with the greatest diffidence and must
not be reckoned on for our spiritual
guidance without the advice of a most

prudent and spiritually enlightened director.

Now, the mystical or higher knowledge of God does not consist in these things. Far from being a kind of vision, all the saints are agreed that it is a blind apprehension or blind perception of God. Such is their doctrine, particularly that expounded by St. John of the Cross, who is no small authority on the subject.

What is meant by a blind perception? We will take, for example, a blind man. He gropes his way about in a perpetual darkness, but does he not hear if spoken to? Does he not feel if objects or persons close at hand come into contact with him? Does he not taste the sweetness of food and drink when given to him? And does he not rejoice at the beneficent warmth of the sun in summer, or of a fire in winter, though he be never so blind? His, then, is what we may call a blind perception. This is precisely what takes place in a spiritual way in the mystical knowledge of God; this is the sort of apprehension of God which the loving soul experiences. Though he does not see God's countenance—for that is given to the blessed in Heaven alone—the mystic nevertheless hears His loving voice in the secret of his heart; he feels the warm embrace of God around him; from time to time he tastes inwardly the sweetness of his consolations; and at all times, even in darkness and tribulation, he feels the strength of God's mighty arm supporting him.

Now, there can be no illusion in this, precisely because it is a blind apprehension of God, and the senses and the imagination have no part in it. It takes place in the most secret part of the soul, where the evil one can have no access to work his wiles. If it were a vision it might be an hallucination of the brain, the work of the prince of darkness; but here there is no image, no representation of any figure or form, no speech heard of the ear. The author of the "Imitation of Christ" is emphatic in insisting that God makes Himself heard to the faithful soul without noise of words (Book i., ch. 3; Book iii., ch. 2). There is no delusion, nor possibility of delusion, in the mystical knowledge of God.

Is the mystic always able accurately to account for his new knowledge of God? No, he is not always conscious of it. He certainly could not put it into words, and he does not care to do so; he does not care to speak of it. He keeps his secret, or rather the secret of the King, well. He loves: that is enough for him.

This blind perception of God, or God known to the mystic by a blind perception, is what spiritual writers call "the Divine Cloud" or the "Dark Night," "la Grande Ténèbre," because of the total absence of all images or figures and the failure of creatures to help therein. The naked soul is alone with God. The universe of things visible and invisible is banished, and ultimately the consciousness, even of self, becomes, for the time being, obliterated.

Thus, at times of mental prayer, the soul, not seeing its God, and yet having lost sight of creatures, is engulfed in a very great darkness. This darkness is God Himself, the very substance of God. A palpable darkness, but not in the earthly sense of the expression. A luminous darkness, dazzling to the eyes of the soul, as the light of day is darkness dazzling to the eyes of the bat or the owl. A wholesome, warm, delectable, desirable darkness, brighter infinitely than the brightest day of creatures, be it even that of the intellect as such. And there can be no illusion in it, no going astray or losing oneself in it, except in the blessed sense indicated by our Lord. *He that shall lose his soul shall find it* (*Matt. x., 39*).

We shall have more to say of this darkness as we proceed. Suffice it to say now that he who begins fervently to love just steps into the Divine Cloud, and he who makes progress in fervent love goes deeper into it; and he who is perfect in fervent love goes deepest into it. On the contrary, he who has not yet begun fervently to love God has not begun truly to know Him: he has not come to the edge of the Divine Cloud. This is, alas! how matters stand with many souls.

It is late in the day. *Novissima hora est (1 Jo. ii., 18)*. Let us begin at once. Let us love God without any fear whatever of the consequences. Let us love God and never fear that such a love will be to us a snare and a delusion. *The Lord is my light and my salvation, whom shall I fear? (Ps. xxvi., 1).*

PART II. OF ENLARGING OUR MYSTICAL KNOWLEDGE OF GOD

"That you may be able to comprehend with all the saints what is the breadth and length and height and depth, that you may be filled with the fulness of God."

Eph. iii., 18, 19.

CHAPTER V

WHAT IT REALLY MEANS

DO the saints during their pilgrimage on earth, or even those in heaven who see God face to face, comprehend the breadth and length and height and depth of God? Do they receive the fulness of Him in themselves? In a way they do, or else the Apostle would not pray that it be granted to his beloved Ephesians; and yet when we consider that God is a Spirit, and therefore has no dimensions, no breadth and length, no height and depth—that being infinite He cannot be held within the limits of any created capacity—we are warned to look for a spiritual, mysterious meaning to these words. For this reason let us consider what is really meant by enlarging our mystical knowledge of God.

Human language is a poor instrument when used to express the mysteries of God. It is wholly inadequate, clumsy, and treacherous; but as it is all we have, we must perforce make use of it, being careful to do so cautiously, and to qualify, if need be, the meaning of our words.

Here, for instance, we speak of enlarging our knowledge of God. Now, there is no such thing as enlarging our knowledge of God. Why then do we use the expression at all? For want of a better one. It conveys our meaning, and yet at the same time it perverts and betrays it. It brings with it a notion that does not fit the nature of God and of God's knowledge. Yet we have no better word for our meaning, and it must serve.

The mystic's knowledge of God is not enlarged as knowledge of other things is enlarged. If, for instance, we speak of enlarging our knowledge of English, we mean more words,

more rules of grammar, more con-
struction and analysis of phrase and
sentence. Of history, more names of
great men, dates of great events, of
battles, revolutions, and treaties of
peace, etc. Of astronomy, more stars
and constellations. To extend one's
knowledge in these matters means a
multiplicity of notions, an extension
in surface, a reaching out to more
things. Not so an increase in the
knowledge of God. This does not
gain in surface, nor does it make for
multiplicity of notions, but, on the
contrary, for simplicity and unity.

This seems subtle and difficult to
understand, but it is a most beautiful
truth. To enlarge one's knowledge of
God, more especially the mystical
knowledge of God, does not mean to
know more things about God, but to
know the one thing, God, more.
This is done in a manner void of

images and creatures, by a simple, intense, and disengaged apprehension of God, Who is absolutely, infinitely pure and simple, of Him Who has said: *I am Who am. (Exod. iii., 14)*.

St. Denys, the Areopagite, who is considered the greatest authority on mystical theology, speaks of the double process by which the human mind seeks to form a true notion of God—namely, the affirmative process and the negative process. By the former we consider all the things of the universe in their beauty and goodness, and we say: "God is this, but in an infinite degree." Thus God is life, light, beauty, power, but in an infinite degree. By the latter we deny that God is anything we can see, or comprehend or conceive. This latter, St. Denys maintains, brings us nearer to the truth, for it leaves us only with a simple apprehension of God, and is

more worthy of His infinite majesty.
It is here—that is to say, at the
acknowledgment, conscious or uncon-
scious, of God's incomprehensibility—
that the soul enters into what St. Denys
calls the Divine Cloud or Darkness,
for now, indeed, the human mind is
dazzled by the brightness of the splen-
dour of God's truth, and is enveloped
in darkness. Blessed is this darkness,
and it were far better here to grope
in blind and loving faith than to
bask in the brightest light of human
reasoning.

The same doctrine is set forth by
St. Thomas in Tract LX. He repre-
sents to us the loving soul thirsting
after God, drinking at all the foun-
tains of created knowledge, and saying
to each one that she drinks from:
"No, ah, no! You are not that which
I am seeking for. You cannot refresh
me! The light of the sun and of the

stars, and the beauty of nature: no, you are not my God! The greatness and the power of the elements: no, you are not my God! The loveliness of man, woman or child: you are not my God!" The saint goes on through all the things that, in the order of creation, might satisfy the soul, but is obliged to confess that nothing, either here below or in heaven above, can bring happiness or give a true idea of what God is, save only God Himself.

But the soul that is in ignorance, the worldly soul, what does she say? To gold and silver and the things of earth, she says: "You are my gods. I love you. You reign supreme in all my thoughts. I delight in you. Surely you will give me happiness." Like the Hebrews of old at the foot of Mount Sinai before the golden calf. *These are thy gods, O Israel! (Exode xxxii., 4).* So does the sinner say to the creatures of flesh and blood, formed of the slime of the earth, things of a day, that will rot on the morrow: " These are my gods ! Would that I might enjoy them here, on this earth, for ever ! " It is thus, alas ! that the devil interposes himself in God's place, and is worshipped as God. Did he not say to our Divine Lord Himself : *All these* (the pleasures and honours of this world) *will I give thee, if, falling down, thou wilt adore me (Mat. iv., 9).*

Comparatively few there are who answer with Our Lord, " The Lord thy God shalt thou adore, and Him only shalt thou serve." To the false gods of the world which can never satisfy, how many there are who sacrifice all : talent, honour, health, time, fortune, body and soul, and even the souls of others dependent on them. Does not treason such as this, if unrepented, throw a lurid light on the reality of hell fire?

But to return to the consideration of the knowledge of God, and of enlarging it by an increase in depth and intensity of the perception of God.

When St. Paul prays that we may be able to comprehend, with the saints, what is the breadth and length, and height and depth, and that we may be filled with the fulness of God, he means two things: the illumination of the mind in regard to Divine mysteries, especially the mystery of the Divine Essence, and a greater fulness of the effects of the presence of God in the secret part of the soul. Indeed, at each new act of Divine contemplation one's notion of God becomes more simple, more ineffable, nearer to the mode of perception of the pure spirits—that is to say, of the angels and souls that are separate from their bodies.

The spiritual experiences of a soul wholly abandoned to God succeed each other with an astounding variety and number.

In the life of St. Angela of Foligno, what strikes one particularly is how each manifestation of God is so marvellous to her that it throws in the shade or blots out entirely all those that preceded it. The saint is at a loss to express her admiration of this effect of God's love. Something similar to this takes place in the mystic soul. It is as though God presented one aspect of His Divine Goodness to her and then withdrew it, saying, " Not this, it is not this," and then another aspect, and withdrew it also, saying again, " Nay, not this, it is not this."

At every fresh mystical experience

the perception of God becomes clearer, more evident, more sweet, more penetrating, and yet less and less demonstrable, just because it is so intimate! It works its way through unknown paths into the depths of inner consciousness, and nothing is able to shake the assurance of the soul that God is there, and that she touches Him, and is being acted upon by Him in a way that is altogether different from that previous to her entrance into the mystic life. Now, this is the way the mystical knowledge of God can be said to enlarge.

In reality, what takes place is this: God is working that precious material, the mystic soul, which has become plastic and passive in His hands. He is scooping it out, pressing it from inside, and, as it were, extending its walls and boundaries.

First, He empties it of self and

all things else, and makes it absolutely clean, and then He makes it larger and larger, and takes possession of it, filling it with His own fulness. By each fresh spiritual experience, the soul grows more and more capable of tasting how sweet her Lord is. By each Divine touch she is made more pure, more refined, more akin to God, more able to enjoy Him. At the same time she becomes more trustful, familiar, and childlike in her dealings with her Beloved. The soul has now become more dead to self and the world, and more responsive to the least touch of the Holy Spirit.

That is what is really meant by enlarging one's mystical knowledge of God.

CHAPTER VI.

HOW WE FAIL TO ENLARGE OUR MYSTICAL KNOWLEDGE

" I will arise and go to my Father."
—Luke xv., 18.

HOW does it happen that the mystical knowledge that comes by love remains, for the greater part of Christians, but rudimentary and undeveloped? How is it that we have so little of that " intimate, conscious, constant union with God " which is the outcome of true love, and which constitutes the mystic life? Whose fault is it? God's or our own? Has God perchance failed to make advances to us and to show us the way? I answer emphatically, No! The good God has made loving advances to us, for there is not one of us who has not tasted, at some time or other, that God is sweet. It may have been when we made our first

Communion, either on the day itself or after. At other times, again and again, God has allured us by making us feel the joy of being near Him, and conversing with Him heart to heart. Who has not had such spiritual experiences, and, after all, when we look back upon our past life, are they not the happiest? Even Napoleon I., at the height of his glory, confessed to his astonished generals that the happiest memory of all his eventful life was that of the day of his first Communion.

In reality, then, we have all had a taste and a beginning of the higher knowledge of God, the mystical, experimental knowledge, communicated directly into the soul by God Himself. A taste and a beginning, but nothing more. Why is this?

Because we have not kept up the loving intercourse with God to which we were invited. We are to blame; the fault is ours.

If we wish to know a person intimately, we are not satisfied with merely becoming acquainted with that person; we seek to keep up our intercourse with him. Having met a man for the first time and had a little conversation with him, and taken stock of him, we are said to have struck up an acquaintance. Should we meet the man the next day, we should recognise him immediately and be recognised by him, and quite naturally resume our intercourse. No more preliminaries would be needed, no fresh introductions necessary. But if, after having met a man once, and spoken with him, for some reason or other we do not wish to meet him again, if he should avoid us and we him, if, for instance, when passing in the street, we turn away from one another, and have nothing to do with one another, then our first acquaintance cannot be said to develop. The memory of it will fade away into the distant past.

Later, perhaps, if the man is mentioned to us, we may remember him, but the memory will bring with it nothing but displeasure, as though this person had injured us, or is it that we feel we were not all we might have been to him?

But if, after our first meeting, we try to meet him again, and again, and again, and each time converse as long as we can and as familiarly as we can, and do all in our power to cultivate his friendship and to please him; and if, on his part, he lays himself open to be known and loved by us, and shows himself to us without restraint, or disguise; if he opens his heart to us, and has no secret from us, then indeed our acquaintance can be said to have developed into a very real friendship. And should the man be good, the more we see of him the more we shall like him, and the more he sees we appreciate him, so much the more will he love us in return. Thus mutual affection will increase and grow in tenderness and strength, and its effect for good will influence our whole life.

If this be the case with poor human love and friendship, what may we not hope of the Divine? The more we endeavour to come near to God, speaking with Him in the secret of our heart, the more He will make Himself known to us, and, on the other hand, the more appreciative we are of His Divine goodness and the more we strive to cultivate His Friendship, so much the more will He love us in return. Then will He unfold to us the treasures of His Heart. Then shall we be permitted to feel the marvellous charms of His sacred Humanity, and the infinite sweetness of His Divinity. As that great lover of God, St. Augustine, says: "God makes Himself to be our honey, and makes us to be His honey." His honey, his delight! And has not God Himself said: *My delights are to be with the children of men?* (Prov. viii. 31). In the Canticle of Canticles, the Heavenly Bridegroom speaks these words to the loving soul: *I am come into my garden, O my sister and spouse. . . . I have eaten the honeycomb with my honey. I have drunk my wine with my milk: eat, O friends, and drink and be inebriated, my dearly beloved.* (Cant. v. 1.). The honey is the soul in which he takes His delight, the honeycomb is the body in which that soul is lodged, as honey in the comb; for the body itself, the flesh and the senses, become affected by the love of God, and, so to say, consumed thereby. The wine which Jesus drinks with the milk typifies the burning charity and sinlessness of the loving soul; and He calls upon His Divine Father and the Holy Ghost, and the blessed Angels and Saints to partake of His joy, as is seen by the words: "Eat, O friends, and drink and be inebriated, O my beloved."

This is the interpretation given by St. Bernard and other Fathers of this passage in the most mystical book of Holy Writ, and from it we may gather to what honour the soul is raised, which follows up her first acquaintance with God and Our Lord Jesus Christ.

We know now why it is that our mystical knowledge of God has remained undeveloped and has borne no fruit. Through no fault on the part of God was it arrested in its beginnings. Loving intercourse by means of mental prayer has not been kept up. We may be in a state of grace, receive the Sacraments and say customary prayers; we have not opened to Him the floodgates of our soul, nor allowed all our affections to flow forth impetuously unto Him, to receive in return the inflowing of His loving tenderness: no wonder we remain in dryness and far from God!

Let us go a step further and ask: Why did we not keep up and develop our first acquaintance with God, by love? Now, it is not always out of indifference or levity that a soul of good-will is arrested on its way to God. Sometimes it is through a lamentable mistake, because what concerns the mystical life is not known or understood. Hence it happens that after the first visitings of God to the soul, the reaction which inevitably follows, plunging the soul into dryness and darkness, surprises her, and causes her to be tempted to abandon the whole enterprise of the spiritual life. She is inclined to think she has made a mistake in aiming so high, and is not called to the ways of the life of love. This season of spiritual darkness, after all, is as natural and as much in order in the spiritual life as day and night, summer and winter, in the physical life of the world. Therefore, should there be someone at hand to tell this soul of goodwill that all is well, and there is no mistake, and that she has only to persevere strenuously in her enterprise: God in his own good time will show her the light again, and revisit her with His consolation.

But again it happens, and this, alas! more often, that the soul has indeed rejoiced at the sweetness of her first meeting with God in the secret of her heart, but that she is not disposed to make the necessary efforts required to keep up this loving intercourse. Mercenary, selfish, ungenerous soul, who would turn her back on God the moment He ceases to pour out upon her His sweetness and consolation. Such a soul as this loves God only for what she can get from Him and so long as He gives her gifts, and not a minute longer. What God gives she loves, but not God for Himself. A very, very low standard of the spiritual life this, and perhaps, if we look well into it, we shall find it to be our own. Small wonder, then, if we go no further than the rudimentary stage in the mystical knowledge of God.

What then is to be done? Change completely our way of acting. Seek out God, and call upon Him, and strive to be ever mindful of His presence. Let us as often as we can enter into the secret chamber of our heart and speak with Him and listen to Him; let us enter resolutely upon the way of love. There need be no fear that the good God will hold aloof from us. A man whom we had so neglected after he had made advances to us, desiring to live with us on terms of friendship, might behave thus. He might reproach us, saying: "What, you come to me after all you have done?" He might thrust the past upon us and turn his back upon us. A man, yes, but the good God, never! Though we have neglected Him in the past, we need not now mistrust Him. We may go back to Him, and we shall find that sooner or later He will welcome us, and lavish on us His treasures.

The story of the Prodigal Son does not only apply to great sinners, but also to tepid and negligent Christians, who have turned away from the loving embraces of their Heavenly Father in the mystical life, and squandered a fortune of time, and grace, and opportunities of becoming saints. They have eaten the husks of the swine, which are their vain desires and self-love, and they are spiritually starving and in rags. Let them say with the prodigal: "I will arise, and I will go to my Father, never to leave Him again, never more to stop my loving intercourse with Him."

CHAPTER VII

HOW IT MAY BE DONE

" The path of the just, as a shining light, goeth forwards and increaseth to perfect day."—Prov. iv. 18.

THE first way in which we can gain a greater mystical knowledge of God is, of course, by direct intercourse with Him in the secret of our heart. This is done by keeping up the loving intercourse with Him as long as possible, as long as our necessary occupations will allow, as long as our fervour lasts and we feel drawn to it. It is not wise at times of spiritual fervour to turn away from God to talk to creatures; to say, "My half-hour of meditation is over, I will now stop this loving intercourse with God." No; if possible, if there is nothing to hinder, it ought to be kept up, even as we go to and fro on our different duties in the day, as long as God is pleased to draw us to Him and give us to taste and see how sweet He is. No measure of time, neither day nor night, ought to restrain us from the loving embrace of God. Nothing, therefore, except the Will of God Himself, made manifest by the call of duty, obedience, or charity, should stay the outflowing of the soul in love and the inflowing of the love of God into the soul. He that is being entertained at the table of the King, will he turn away to revel with menials and mendicants? He who finds a great treasure of golden coins and precious stones and has but to gather them in, will he waste his time in picking up pebbles and brass buttons? Will the thirsty man who has found a fountain of pure fresh water, turn aside to drink out of a puddle a few drops of stagnant, poisoned water?

And when at last this loving,

direct intercourse with the Beloved comes to an end, as it will do from time to time in our present condition, let us be eager, let us try to renew it, watching and being ready to seize upon the first occasion, the first motion of grace.

But even when we are quite willing and eager to keep up the loving intercourse with God in the secret of our heart, there are times when, try as we may, we are unable to come into touch with the Beloved. We know He is there, in our heart (He is always there), we try to speak with Him, but we fail to get any response. A season of spiritual dryness has set in and this may last a very long time. The good God does not show us His loving countenance, nor let us hear His voice, as of yore, nor does He fill us with the sweetness which so delighted us. What are we to do?

We must love Him as much in dryness as in refreshment, and humbly bless Him. Let us say with holy Job: *The Lord gave, and the Lord hath taken away . . . blessed be the nameo f the Lord* (Job i. 21), and then bravely pursue our efforts at advancing in the knowledge of God. For this purpose we may turn to the Holy Scriptures.

As one deprived of the loved presence of a friend reads and re-reads his letters, and dwells fondly upon passages he had not noticed at first or had lost sight of, and thus enlarges his knowledge of the absent friend, so, *by patience, and the consolation of the Scriptures* (Rom. xv. 4), by piously and thoughtfully reading and re-reading the Gospels and the other parts of the Bible, we shall enlarge our mystical knowledge of God.

But we must read, not for the sake

of mere human learning, nor out of curiosity, but for love alone. Such reading ought to be undertaken at all times and by all, no matter in what sphere of life they may be called to labour. If we read the Scriptures with the eager desire of gaining some golden particles of the mystical knowledge of God, we shall assuredly find therein treasures and untold wealth. For, there, God has portrayed Himself in human language, making use of our modes of thought and expression: for love, He has here accommodated Himself to our small capacity, as a fond parent stoops down to a little babe and stammers and babbles with it in a childish way.

Our previous experience in the mystic life, our loving intercourse with God, will throw an intense light upon texts of Holy Writ which otherwise would have failed to arrest our attention. The very words of God will now enlighten us as to His dealings with our soul, and enable us to understand His ways.

Thus we may enlarge our mystical knowledge of God, at times when we are unable to do so by direct intercourse.

There is yet another way.

We want to know more about God? Let us go to the creatures of the earth whom He has fashioned, and who can speak of Him. Let us seek Him in Creation; let us contemplate Him lovingly in the magnificence of the universe: the sun by day, the stars by night, the earth and the sea, all life and motion, light, joy, beauty, all these are his witnesses! *The Heavens show forth the glory of God, and the firmament declareth the work of His hands* (Ps. xix. 1). The birds sing of his loving kindness. The tiniest flower of the field, more gorgeously arrayed than Solomon in all his glory, tells of the tender providence of the Father in Heaven. The very stones have a voice and proclaim Him, and, in listening and being attentive to these voices, our knowledge and our love of the good God will grow in depth and intensity. A saint used to stroke the flowers gently with his staff, and say : " Ah, hold your peace, you chide me, you cry out the excess of the love of God! " Then there are those who can speak of Him in our own language, and tell us about Him, because they have known Him : I mean His intimate friends, the saints. In times of dryness, let us read what the saints have written about God, and let us also read the lives of the saints. Let us, in preference to all others, choose those writers whose names are prefixed by Holy Church with the letter S. or B., "Saint" or "Blessed." They are the graduates of the spiritual life; they have their sheepskins, so to speak, their parchments, their degrees; they have been proved and found worthy. They speak with the truth, simplicity, and authority to which mere scholarship could never attain, because they have experienced the life of which they write.

St. John, in his first Epistle, says: *That which was from the beginning, which we have heard, which we have seen with our eyes, which we have looked upon and our hands have handled, of the word of life .... we declare unto you* (1. Jo. i. 1-3). These same words the saints and holy writers may justly use in a sense but slightly different. And studying their lives we see how in all things, without ceasing, they applied themselves to God—how their souls were poured out in loving intercourse with Him, and how He met them in a loving embrace. And in this way again we become conversant in the ways of God, and understand His divine operations.

CHAPTER VIII

"THE LAST WORD ABOUT IT ALL"

ST. THOMAS AQUINAS in his youth was insistently asking of his teachers the one question: "What is God? What is He in Himself? In His true self?" To this question human reason ever seeks to give some sort of answer, but after a good deal of stammering, it is obliged to confess: "I do not know. I have not seen God in Himself, but only His reflection dimly mirrored in His works. I cannot conceive what He is in Himself, much less express Him in words of human speech." Even the assertions of reason, that God is the first Cause, the Creator of heaven and earth, or that He is a pure Spirit, do not tell us what manner of being He is. The devil, for that matter, is a pure spirit.

We turn to Faith, Christian Faith, and we ask her to tell us what God is in Himself, and Faith has an answer ready: "God is the Blessed Trinity, Father, Son, and Holy Ghost, Three Persons in One Divine Essence"; and Faith is sure that hers is the right answer, for God Himself has dictated it. But, for all that, Faith does not comprehend what she professes. This is a mystery, the very greatest of mysteries. Faith does but repeat the words she has learnt, with the docility of a child repeating a lesson, but she is like the child who often does not fully understand what he repeats. So that even Faith cannot give a satisfying answer to our question, "What is God?"

Now, love will try his turn. He, of all others, is eager to know what God is. He pushes rapidly beyond all the things of this world, visible

and invisible, for he knows they cannot tell him. He hears and hearkens
to the answer of Faith, but he is not
satisfied. He pushes forward, boldly
and blindly, for he cannot see his
object, but he will find his answer ;
it will offer itself to him. When God
sees a soul in quest of Him, He
meets her, ah, more than half-way.
Seek and you shall find. Love meets
his object. He grapples with it
in the darkness of this mortal life,
and he forces its secret out : " Tell
me, what art Thou ? " The answer
comes straight from God Himself,
not by words of human speech, but
by a burning impression of His own
Divine substance upon the substance
of the soul, wherein He gives her to
know what He is. *God is Charity.*

The answer has been given. The
soul, like Jacob wrestling with the
angel, has been bold enough to ask :

"By what name art Thou called?"
And she has received an answer
sharper than a two-edged sword. The
poor, loving soul is wounded by the
Divine touch. From now she feels she
will never be able to go through life
with the same assured step as before.
She will halt and reel as one in pain
or as a drunken person, and in truth
she is both drunken and in pain—
drunken with the delight, the perfume,
the substantial joy of knowing God to
be charity ; and groaning and in pain
at the weight of the mighty revelation.
The stricken soul can say but one
thing : God is Charity, *Deus charitas
est!* and the world thinks this person
must be mad. Have not all the saints,
one after another, passed in the eyes
of the world for madmen, and their
Master before them ?

But, you may say, we know this.
We have in St. John, I. Ep., ch. iv.

16, *God is Charity*. Macaulay would say the merest schoolboy knows this. Where is the difference between our knowledge and that of the mystic? The difference is this. "God is Charity" is an article of abstract faith for the mere theologian; for the mystic, it is a living fact. A living fact, glowing and resplendent as the sun in heaven. A fact which he feels in himself, in his own soul and body, with as much personal, experimental knowledge as we have of the sun above our heads on a midsummer day.

Yes, we may read in Holy Writ the words, "God is Charity," and repeat them, and give a learned demonstration of them, and all the while they may be to us nothing more than the statement of a truth which makes no impression on us. This is a light, a light of a kind, subdued and cold, as that of the distant stars. But these same words that leave the philosopher or the theologian cold and loveless, negligent and mayhap in mortal sin, will set the true servant of God all aglow and on fire.

A frigid observer, himself perishing of cold, might be able to analyse and describe accurately how it is that the property of fire is to burn. The charcoal in the fire cannot describe anything, yet it does better, it burns. It shows the process in its very self, even causing to flame up and burn what comes into contact with it. So it is with the mystic. He may be unable to put his perception of God into words, define it, or reason it out. But he apprehends so vividly that God is love, by actual contact, that he is himself set all on fire with love. This knowledge seems, as it were, to transform the mystic into the very substance of the love of God.

The greatest proof of the reality and non-delusion of the knowledge of God by love is that it calls out, in the mystic soul, love in its highest degree. The whole conduct of the saint or mystic (for we must remember that the true mystic is a saint) proclaims the truth that God is love, just as the conduct of the charcoal thrown into the flames proclaims the fact that fire is a burning and consuming element. The hatred of the loving soul for self, her indifference to all the world, excepting in direct reference to the love of God, her turning away from creatures and her complete abandonment to God, her loving attention to the presence of God and joy in the thought of Him, show forth that she has indeed a vivid, vital apprehension of God under this

His most enthralling aspect—Charity.

All this takes place in the mystic, the saint, the true servant of God, whether he be literate or illiterate. Whatever his natural endowments or limitations, the mystic is made to feel by immediate contact that God is love, all love, nothing but love, love in three Divine Persons. He is made to realise experimentally that this infinite ocean of love is pressing all around his heart to break into it and make it divinely happy. For him God is a burning sun of love, in the warm light of which the whole world of angels and men, and all inferior creatures, animate and inanimate, are basking, whether they know it or not, as the small gnats and atoms dancing in the rays of the sun.

He knows that God is substantial love, the only love worthy of the heart of man or angel, the only one capable of filling the great yawning void of his heart and its immense desire and capacity for loving and being loved.

All this, whether the mystic be literate or illiterate.

But if he be a learned man, inclined—or, rather, moved by the Holy Spirit—to write on the subject, then the world is the gainer. Then shall we have such works as the " Confessions and Soliloquies " of St. Augustine, St. Bernard's " Sermons on the Canticles," " The Third Book of the Imitation of Christ," " The Living Flame of Love " of St. John of the Cross, " The Treatise on the Love of God," by St. Francis of Sales, to name but a few. The mystic of learning and genius is made to see, and is able to show as no one else, the love of God, in all the pages of Holy Writ, in all the mysteries of religion, in all the events of history, in all the circumstances of his own life and that of others, precisely because the very love that God is in Himself is burning bright in the very centre of his soul, illuminating it and all things else for him.

Here, then, is our question answered. This is the last word about God—final in time and eternity: God is Love. If we say: "God is Good, God is Life, God is Light"; if we say: "God is the Creator of heaven and earth, He is our Father in heaven, He gave us His only Son, He pours out His Holy Spirit upon all flesh," we mean only God is Love. And when we shall have come to the Beatific Vision in heaven we shall perceive that to be the ineffable Trinity, to be the Father, Son, and Holy Ghost, is a law of the substantial love of God. Then at last we shall indeed be set on fire with the love of God, and that for all eternity.

EPILOGUE

AS my readers who have had the patience to follow me to the end have no doubt realised, my aim in this booklet has been wholly practical: to fire souls with the love of God and with longing for that special knowledge of God which comes through love alone.

However awkwardly I may have acquitted myself of the task, I hope I shall not be considered presumptuous if I make my own, on behalf of my readers, the beautiful prayer of St. Paul for his beloved Ephesians, Eph. iii. 18.

"I bow my knees to the Father of our Lord Jesus Christ, of Whom all paternity on earth and in heaven is named, that He would grant you according to the riches of His glory, to be strengthened by His Spirit with might unto the inward man; that Christ may dwell by faith in your hearts; that being rooted and founded in charity, you may be able to comprehend, with all the *saints, what is the breadth, and length, and height, and depth, to know also the charity of Christ which surpasseth all knowledge; that you may be filled unto all the fulness of God."*

And finally, dear reader, before we part company, shall we not add also with the same apostle: "Now to Him Who is able to do all things more abundantly than we desire or understand, according to the power that worketh in us, to Him be glory in the Church, and in Christ Jesus unto all generations, world without end. Amen."

Made in the USA
San Bernardino, CA
23 July 2019